Thomas Edison

THE MAN WHO INVENTED hELLO

FLIP BOOK

AN EARLY EDISON FILM

LET THERE BE LIGHT

CHIEF OF THE INSOMNIA SQUAD

OVER 1,000 INVENTIONS

Genius!

What is genius? According to Thomas Edison, it's 1 percent inspiration and 99 percent perspiration. By this definition, Edison certainly qualified. From childhood to the end of his long life, Edison was always working on some project. Many of them were inspirations that changed the world we live in. The incandescent electric light bulb, the phonograph, the motion picture projector—these are the most famous, but there were many more. In his lifetime, Edison received patents for 1,093 inventions.

Edison was more than an inventor, though. In the interest of seeing his inventions become reality, he had to become a businessman as well. After building the first movie camera, for example, he built a studio on the grounds of his West Orange, New Jersey, laboratory and produced the first motion pictures.

Edison was far from the stereotype of the antisocial inventor who shuns society to follow his inner vision. More than any other inventor, he created the modern team approach to research and development of new ideas. You might say, it was an unpatented invention.

Where did Edison get his inspirations, and just how much perspiration did it take to see his dreams become reality? Read on as *Kids Discover* takes you on a journey with a genius.

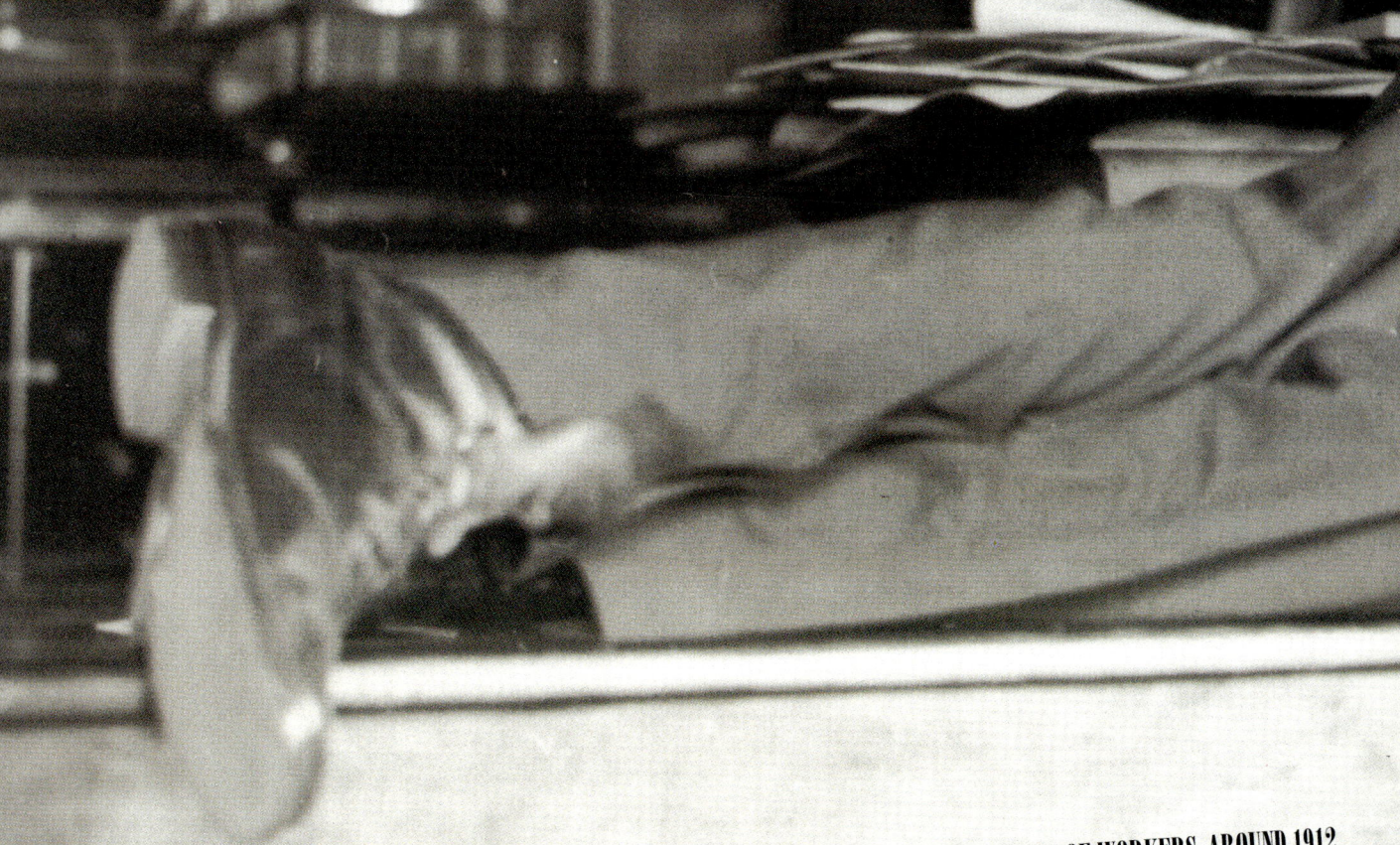

EDISON AND HIS COLLEAGUES WERE KNOWN TO WORK 24 HOURS A DAY. IN FACT, A SPECIFIC GROUP OF WORKERS, AROUND 1912, CALLED THEMSELVES "THE INSOMNIA SQUAD." CATNAPS—SOME TAKEN ON A LABORATORY BENCH—KEPT EDISON REFRESHED.

◀ **EDISON'S CIRCLE OF** friends included many famous people. Here are (from left to right) Edison, Harvey S. Firestone, Jr., naturalist John Burroughs, automaker Henry Ford, Harvey S. Firestone, founder of the Firestone Tire and Rubber Co., and (seated) R.J.H. de Loach at a waterwheel in West Virginia.

1847 • THE EDISON ERA • 1931

As a boy in Milan, Ohio, Edison wondered at the sight of covered wagons carrying pioneers westward. By the time Edison died in 1931, Charles Lindbergh had made the first solo transatlantic flight in an airplane. Between 1847 and 1931, the United States was transformed from a largely rural and agricultural society to an urban, industrialized one. Inventive advances in transportation, communication, and manufacturing made it happen. Edison may have been the most prolific inventor of his age, but he wasn't the only one. Here are some other people's inventions.

▶ **TEN YEARS** before Edison's birth, Samuel F. B. Morse introduced a new way of communicating. Before the telegraph, there were two ways to get a message across the country: by horse-drawn stagecoach or by ship around Cape Horn. It could take weeks to get a letter from one coast to the other. With Morse's invention, messages, coded as dots and dashes, traveled as electrical impulses over wires in a matter of minutes. As a boy, Edison was fascinated with telegraphy. He and a friend rigged up a primitive telegraph between their houses and taught themselves Morse code. Some of Edison's first inventions were improvements on the telegraph.

▼ **A BRITISH** invention, the steam locomotive began its first regularly scheduled operation in the United States on Christmas Day 1830. By 1850, 9,000 miles of track had been laid, and by 1880, there were 93,000. The first transcontinental railroad was finished in 1869. Trains created an economic revolution, making more goods available to more people. They also opened up the Great Plains and Rocky Mountain plateau to settlers.

"THE GREATEST INVENTION OF THE NINETEENTH CENTURY WAS THE INVENTION OF THE METHOD OF INVENTION."
★ ★ ALFRED NORTH WHITEHEAD ★ ★

▲ **IN 1876, WHILE** trying to create an efficient hearing aid, Alexander Graham Bell fashioned a device that eventually made instantaneous long-distance communication available to everyone. The first telephone was a primitive instrument into which people had to shout to make themselves heard. In 1877, Edison improved the telephone's sound transmission by developing a carbon button for the transmitter. Edison was also the first person to use "Hello" when answering the telephone.

▲ **IN 1885,** German Karl Friedrich Benz produced the first successful gasoline-powered automobile. Eight years later, the Duryea brothers made the first car in the U.S. But it was Henry Ford, encouraged by his friend Thomas Edison, who brought this culture-changing form of transportation to the masses. In 1908, he introduced the Model T, a no-frills automobile that sold for under a thousand dollars. By developing the assembly-line method of manufacturing, Ford was able to lower the price of the Model T to $290 by 1925.

▲ **RADIO WAVES** were discovered in 1888. By 1890, Italian Guglielmo Marconi was experimenting with using them to send messages over long distances. In 1906, the first voices and music were sent over the radio. In 1920, KDKA began regularly scheduled broadcasts from the studio above in Pittsburgh.

▲ **ON DECEMBER** 17, 1903, bicycle-shop owners Wilbur and Orville Wright made the first successful flights in a plane powered by an internal combustion engine. Edison had no connection with the Wright brothers' plane, but he was interested in flight. The story is told that as a child he talked a handyman into drinking carbonated medicine because he knew bubbles were lighter than air. But the experiment never got off the ground, as the handyman was soon doubled over in pain. The medicine was a laxative!

▶ **NOT LONG AFTER** radio became popular, Russian-American Vladimir Zworykin patented the first television camera, which he called an iconoscope. A year later, in 1924, he patented the kinescope, a picture tube. RCA began regular broadcasts in the U.S. in 1936, but World War II halted work on improvements to the TV as all efforts went toward winning the war. So it wasn't until the late 1940s, almost two decades after Edison's death, that television as we know it became a household word.

◀ **THE FIRST STEP** into space was taken just five years before Edison's death, when American inventor Robert Goddard launched the first liquid-fuel rocket. Solid-fuel rockets require oxygen from Earth's atmosphere in order to burn. Because Goddard's rocket contained liquid oxygen, it could burn beyond the atmosphere, making space travel possible.

YOUNG AL

Named Thomas after a great uncle and Alva after a family friend, Thomas Alva Edison was called Al all of his childhood years. He was called other things, too, so the story goes, including "addled" (confused, stupid) by a teacher who didn't understand that young Al Edison learned by asking questions, not by answering them.

Early in life, Edison showed the inquisitive mind—and the experimental bent—of a scientist, sometimes to humorous effect, sometimes with near-disastrous results. Though the accuracy of many stories about his childhood has been questioned, there may be an

▲ **THE EDISON** family had originally emigrated from Holland to New Jersey. When the Revolutionary War broke out, they took the British side. Afterward, they fled to Canada to avoid the wrath of their neighbors. Thomas Edison's father became involved in a revolutionary movement against the Canadian government. In 1837, when the rebellion was crushed, he fled for his life to the United States.

▲ **FROM THE AGES** of seven to nine, Al Edison attended three different schools (including the one above) in his new hometown of Port Huron, Michigan. His teachers had no patience with Al's learning style—his endless questions and his apparent inability to sit still. Finally, his mother, who had been a teacher before her marriage, decided to homeschool him.

"Somewhere between the ages of eleven and fifteen, the average child begins to suffer from an atrophy, the paralysis of curiosity and the suspension of the power to observe. The trouble I should judge to lie with the schools."
—Thomas Alva Edison

▲ **THOMAS EDISON** was born in this house on February 11, 1847, in Milan, Ohio, the youngest of seven children, only four of whom survived to adulthood.

element of truth in some of them. It is said, for example, that when just a young boy, Edison asked why geese sat on eggs. Upon being told that mother geese sat on eggs to keep them warm until they hatched, Al disappeared for several hours. His older sister finally found him sitting on goose eggs, soundly disappointed that none had hatched. Other experiments had more alarming results. At the age of six, intrigued with fire, Al started a small blaze in his father's barn. Wind fanned the flames, and the barn soon burned down. Al escaped the flames, but probably not his father's wrath!

◀ **At the age of** 12, with his dad's help, Al got a job selling newspapers and other travelers' necessities on the Grand Trunk Railroad, which made one six-hour round-trip a day between Port Huron and Detroit. To make good use of his time, Al set up a traveling chemistry lab in the baggage car. After acquiring a printing press, he began publishing a newspaper for the commuters.

▶ **During his** early years, Al had scarlet fever and frequently suffered from ear infections. Later in life, he had a severe hearing impairment. Most biographers trace this to his childhood ailments, but Edison told two different stories—both involving the same railroad conductor. He said that when a chemical spill caused a fire in the baggage-car laboratory, the conductor boxed his ears before throwing him off the train. The other story was that once when Edison was running to catch the train with his arms full of newspapers, the conductor helped him aboard by grabbing onto the only part of Edison he could reach—his ears.

While working for the railroad, Al made a flying leap just in time to push the stationmaster's child out of the path of an oncoming freight car. The stationmaster was so grateful that he offered to teach Al to become a telegraph operator, a profession that fascinated Al. A delighted Al quit his job with the railroad and became a pupil once again.

First Fruits

Telegraphy didn't come easy to Tom (as Edison began to call himself at the age of 15) because his hearing difficulties made him slow to pick up the dots and dashes coming over the wires. Still, he was soon good enough to support himself at the job. However, Edison was not interested in making a career as a telegrapher. He wanted the chance to experiment with the equipment.

➤ **THE FASTEST** telegraphers got the best jobs, but Edison was not very fast. To give himself an advantage, he invented a way to slow down telegraphy. He hooked together two telegraph machines. The first one recorded the dots and dashes in the form of indentations on a strip of paper. Edison then fed this strip through the second machine, which was slowed down by a clockwork mechanism to less than the original 40 words per minute. This gave Edison a better chance of jotting down messages. This repeating telegraph was the basis of many of Edison's later improvements to the telegraph.

EDISON MADE IMPROVEMENTS TO THE TELEGRAPH

❋ VOTE RECORDER ❋

◀ **EDISON PATENTED** his first invention—an electric vote recorder—at the age of 22, in 1869. His idea was to eliminate the roll call in which legislators stood up one by one to announce their votes on a given bill. Edison never sold one vote recorder. Legislators didn't want their votes recorded automatically. They used the time during voice votes to attempt to persuade fellow legislators to change their votes.

❋ STOCK TICKER ❋

◀ **THOUGH HIS** automatic vote recorder was a financial disaster, Edison quit his job as a telegrapher to devote all of his time to bringing out his inventions. In Boston, he experimented with improvements to stock tickers, which used the principles of telegraphy to electrically record the ever-changing prices of stocks (shares in businesses that are bought and sold publicly). Moving to New York City, Edison met ticker-manufacturer Dr. Samuel Laws, who was so pleased with the improved machines that he handed Edison a check for $40,000.

❖ PHONOGRAPH ❖

◀ **EDISON HAD** already invented a way of recording the clicks of a telegraph message on a strip of paper with a needle. Now he wondered if the sounds transmitted by a telephone's diaphragm (a disk that vibrates with sound waves) could be recorded in the same way. The first phonograph was a cylinder covered with tinfoil soft enough to record the impression of a needle. In 1877, Edison turned the cylinder with a crank and spoke into a diaphragm: "Mary had a little lamb...." When he finished the nursery rhyme, he placed a needle attached to another diaphragm on the cylinder and began to crank. Out came his voice: "Mary had a little lamb...." Much later, Edison used his invention to manufacture talking dolls.

❖ TALKING DOLL ❖

▲ **With the money** he received from Laws, Edison set up his own combination laboratory and factory in Newark, New Jersey. In 1876, he left Newark for the relative quiet of Menlo Park (above), some 12 miles south of Newark. The new laboratory was for research and development. On the second floor were individual workstations amid shelves lined with bottles of chemicals. Many exciting innovations came out of this lab, including the phonograph and the incandescent light bulb. Edison became famous as "the Wizard of Menlo Park." In 1887, he opened his West Orange laboratory (right).

"No experiments are useless."
—Edison

"I'll never give up for I may have a streak of luck before I die."

Edison, July 26, 1869

EDISON SPEAKING INTO the voice tube of the Ediphone. With this dictating device, a person's words were recorded onto a wax cylinder. A typist could then play back the cylinder and type the words onto paper.

Anatomy of an Invention

When cartoonists want to indicate that someone has had a "bright idea," they frequently draw a light bulb over the person's head. This simple graphic image is not only a symbol of enlightenment, it's also a tribute to the genius of Thomas Alva Edison. Edison certainly didn't "invent" electricity. Nor did he create the first electric lighting. But he did find a way to make electric lighting available to homes and offices on a grand scale.

IN 1878, EDISON accompanied a scientific expedition to Wyoming to view a total eclipse of the sun and to use his newly invented tasimeter to measure the heat from the sun's corona during the eclipse. Spurred on by talks with fellow scientists, Edison stated that he would invent a safe, inexpensive electric light to replace the dirty, hazardous kerosene and gas lamps that lit most homes and offices. He envisioned not only an electric light but also a system for delivery of electricity to individual buildings that would make the light useful.

▲ **ONCE ON THE** trail of an idea, Edison spared no expense. Because of his reputation, he was able to get financial backing for his projects. A group of wealthy businessmen formed the Edison Electric Light Company and gave Edison an advance of $30,000 for expenses.

▲ **OVER THE YEARS,** many scientists contributed ideas about electricity. They showed that it flows from object to object, that some objects conduct it better than others, and that lightning is a form of electricity. In 1800, Italian Alessandro Volta (seated, above) made an electric battery. Shortly after, Hans Christian Oersted of Denmark showed that wires carrying electric currents acted like magnets. In 1831, Englishman Michael Faraday showed that magnetism could produce electricity. Faraday's work formed the basis of Edison's work with electricity.

➤ **IN THE EARLY** 1870s, a kind of electric lighting, called arc lighting, had been installed in some outdoor areas. The drawbacks were that it was too bright for indoor use, and the current flowed in one direct line. If one light went out, all the lights in the series went out. Edison's solution was to connect lights in a parallel circuit by subdividing the electric current. If one light failed, the others would be unaffected.

BEFORE EDISON   **AFTER EDISON**

"I owe my success to the fact that I never had a clock in my workroom." —EDISON

THE PUMP UPTON DESIGNED FOR EDISON

▶ **EDISON REALIZED** that to use electricity to produce a glow that would burn for a long time, he needed a filament (thread) that would glow without burning up and a container that had almost no air in it—in other words, a vacuum tube. Hermann Sprengel had designed the first efficient vacuum pump in 1865. However, it was still rare in the U.S. Edison put one of his assistants, Francis Upton, to work on the pump problem.

◀ **TO FIND THE** right filament, Edison resorted to his typical method—trial and error. For a while, he worked exclusively with platinum. Not only were the experiments unsuccessful, but the metal wire was expensive. Eventually Edison returned to his old standby, carbon, plentiful around the Menlo Park lab because of its use in making telephone transmitters. Edison's assistant Charles Batchelor experimented with carbonizing many substances: celluloid, cedar, coconut hair, fish line, and cotton soaked in boiling tar. Eventually, he tried scorching simple cotton thread. On October 22, 1879, Edison and his assistants took turns watching in teams as a bulb with the carbonized thread burned for about 13 1/2 hours. The team had succeeded! They had invented a working electric light bulb.

▼ **THE CARBONIZED** cotton thread worked as a filament, but Edison was not convinced it was the best material. So he kept on experimenting. It wasn't until the summer of 1880 that he settled on carbonized bamboo fiber as the filament of choice.

CHECK IT OUT!
What material is used for the filaments of light bulbs today?
(answer on back cover)

▶ **WHEN EDISON** came up with the carbonized bamboo fiber filament, wealthy backers were relieved that their money had been well spent. Now they wanted to reap the practical rewards of their investment. For over two years, Edison oversaw the building of an electric power station on Pearl Street near New York City's financial district. On September 4, 1882, a switch was pulled, and the first 85 customers of the Edison Electric Illuminating Co. of New York lit their new electric lamps.

Moving Right Along

GOLDENROD: A SOURCE OF RUBBER?

There was something restless in the spirit of Thomas Edison. In 1882, at the age of 35, he shut down his Menlo Park laboratory, and from 1882 to 1887, he worked out of several temporary locations. Finally, in 1887, his base of operations moved to West Orange, New Jersey, where he would live for the rest of his life. There he built a huge laboratory and staffed it with the best minds he could find. Edison would immerse himself completely in a project, sometimes working on it for ten years. He would have to be thoroughly convinced a project wouldn't work before he would give it up. Because he was never quite satisfied, he might institute a change when something was already on the assembly line—much to the dismay of the workers.

▲ **SCIENTISTS HAD** known for some time that the human brain retains an image for at least one-tenth of a second after the image is no longer in view. It stood to reason that if a sequence of photographs could be shot quickly—showing, for example, an animal in a series of movements with only small changes in position—the images would appear to move. But photographs had to be taken one at a time on glass plates. Then George Eastman developed celluloid film that could be quickly pulled through a camera. Using this new, fast-moving film, Edison invented the kinetograph—a motion picture camera —and the kinetoscope—a viewer.

KINETOSCOPE

▲ **AS WITH MANY** of his inventions, Edison threw himself into developing a market for them. Near his West Orange lab, he built the world's first movie studio, called "Black Maria" (left), and turned out the earliest motion pictures. At first they were simple sequences—one of his assistants sneezing or a boxer in action. Later, the studio produced 14-minute comedies and dramas.

▲ **ELECTRIC AUTO-** mobiles came into being in the early part of the century. Between 1899 and 1909, Edison developed a light nickel-iron-alkaline battery. However, electric cars did not catch on then because gasoline was cheap and abundant. Since the batteries needed to be recharged often, the cars couldn't be far from the battery source.

▼ **EDISON INVENTED** an iron-ore separator to remove iron from iron ore. He became convinced that he could remove low-grade iron from lesser quality ores so that mines that were considered used up might still be profitable. This was Edison's one big failure. He was never able to work out the problems with the process.

◀ **EDISON BECAME** head of the Naval Consulting Board in 1915, two years before the United States entered World War I. The U.S. felt it should have a team of scientists to help in case the war hit close to home. Edison directed research on torpedoes (left) and anti-submarines, inventing some 40 defenses against enemy subs. The Navy awarded him the Distinguished Service Medal—the first ever given to a civilian.

EDISON'S LAST project, undertaken in his 80s, was something completely different. He wanted to find a domestic source of rubber—a native American plant producing rubber—to reduce the country's dependence on foreign rubber. At the time of his death in 1931, he thought he had found what he was looking for in a species of goldenrod. However, foreign rubber prices soon dropped, and the desire for domestic rubber declined.

" *Whatever I may have accomplished in my life has been the result of hard persistent labor.* "

—Thomas Edison, objecting to the nickname "Wizard."

THINK PIECE!
Which of Edison's inventions do you think is the most important? Why?

Family and Friends

For much of his life, Edison was the most famous and revered man in America. In his later years, people thronged around him wherever he went. He courted publicity for his inventions, but he was essentially a man who loved solitude.

◀ **IN 1871,** Edison married 16-year-old Mary Stilwell, who worked at his factory in Newark. Because of Edison's long work days, Mary was lonely, and she eventually suffered from emotional instability—some say because of her husband's neglect. Mary bore three children—Marion, nicknamed Dot, Thomas, Jr. (Dash), and William. Mary died in 1884.

◀ **IN 1886,** Edison married another beautiful young woman, 20-year-old Mina Miller. Mina also bore three children—Madeleine, Charles, and Theodore. In the early years, Mina, too, felt neglected. In later years, Mina, emotionally stronger than Mary, made a place for herself in Thomas Edison's busy life.

▶ **THROUGHOUT** his life, Edison depended on the loyalty of key colleagues who worked with him for years, like some of his Menlo Park staff (above, right). Among them were Charles Batchelor, Francis Upton, and John Kruesi, who translated Edison's rough drawings overnight into whatever the "Old Man" wanted.

▶ **AUTOMOBILE** magnate Henry Ford and Edison first met when the young Ford was an employee of the Edison Illuminating Company of Detroit. When they met again, 16 years later, it was more as equals, but Ford never lost his hero worship of the older inventor. Ford wrote: "His knowledge is almost universal. He is interested in every conceivable subject and he recognizes no limitations. He believes all things are possible. At the same time he keeps his feet on the ground. He goes forward step by step…."

▶ **ON OCTOBER 18,** 1931, his body weakened by overwork and poor eating habits, Thomas Edison died. On the night of his funeral, for one minute, all but the most essential lights were dimmed across the country, as Americans paid tribute to the genius who had given them light. At right, people wait for a chance to view Edison's body in his lab.

"It's very beautiful over there." THOMAS EDISON'S LAST WORDS

DOT ⚙ TO ⚙ DOT

Connect the dots to make a picture of Tom Edison on his first job. Then color it.

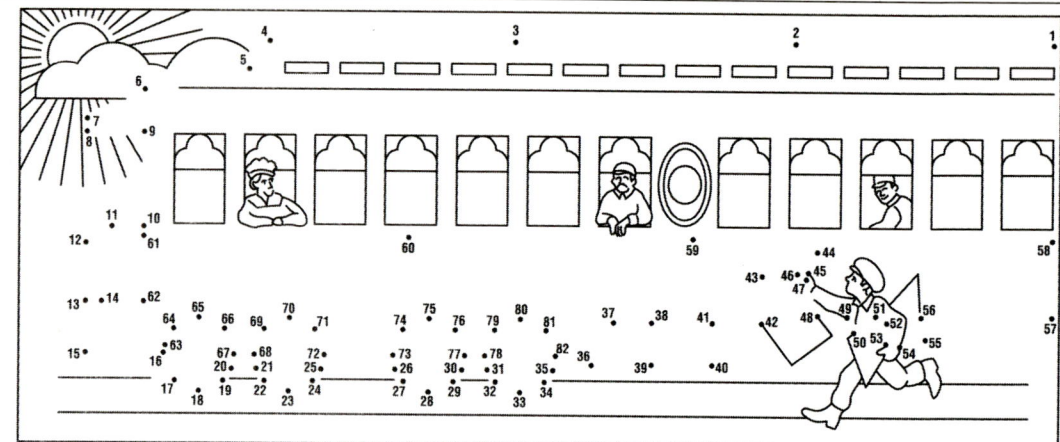

EVERYDAY CHEMISTRY
★ ★

Thomas Edison started his inventing career by doing simple experiments with readily available materials. Here are some simple experiments for you to try.

BLEACH FUN

The bleach used to remove stains from clothing and get clothes whiter is a solution of sodium hypochlorite. When the bleach is added to water (hydrogen and oxygen), the chlorine in the bleach combines with the hydrogen in the water. The oxygen in the water combines with the dirt or stain to form a colorless compound. Here's how to see this in action.

Start with a glass of water. Add enough liquid ink to discolor the water.

While stirring the mixture, add 1 tablespoon of liquid bleach. The water will turn colorless again, as the chemical reaction takes place.

INVISIBLE INK

If life gives you lemons…make invisible ink. The juice of lemons (and other fruits) contains carbon compounds. Mixed with water, the juice is almost colorless. When heated, the compounds break down and release carbon, which is black. You can use this knowledge to write secret messages.

Squeeze some lemon juice into a small bowl. Stir in a few drops of water.

Dip an old-fashioned pen, a thin brush, or a cotton swab into the mixture and write a message on white paper.

When the "ink" is dry, it will be invisible. Hold the paper near a light bulb to heat it and reveal the message.

CLEAN MONEY

Why do pennies get dull? Because oxygen from the air combines with the copper in a penny to form a coating of copper oxide. An acid substance, like lemon or vinegar, will react with the copper oxide to remove the oxygen and make the penny bright again.

Squeeze some lemon juice into a glass. Drop in a penny.

Wait five minutes. Then go fishing for a bright copper penny.